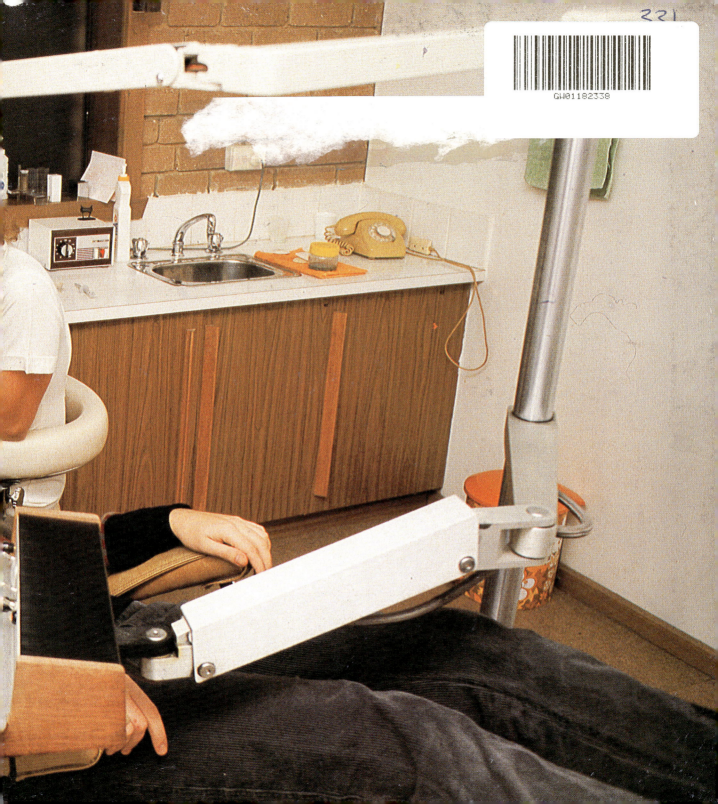

© 1988 Franklin Watts

Franklin Watts
12a Golden Square
London W1

Franklin Watts Australia
14 Mars Road
Lane Cove
N.S.W. 2066

ISBN: 0 86313 648 6

Design: Edward Kinsey
Illustration: Tony Payne

Typesetting: Keyspools Limited
Printed in Italy
by G. Canale & C S.p.A. - Turin

Note: Many of the photographs in this book originally appeared in *Dentist* in the "People" series, also published by Franklin Watts.

DENTIST

Tim Wood
Photographs: Chris Fairclough

Franklin Watts
London/New York/Sydney/Toronto

DERBYSHIRE
COUNTY LIBRARY

Date   3 SEP 1990

....

Class ....

SCHOOL LIBRARY SERVICE

Here is a dentist.
She looks after people's teeth.
She works in a dental surgery.

Two dental nurses help in the surgery. They keep a record card for each patient and make appointments.

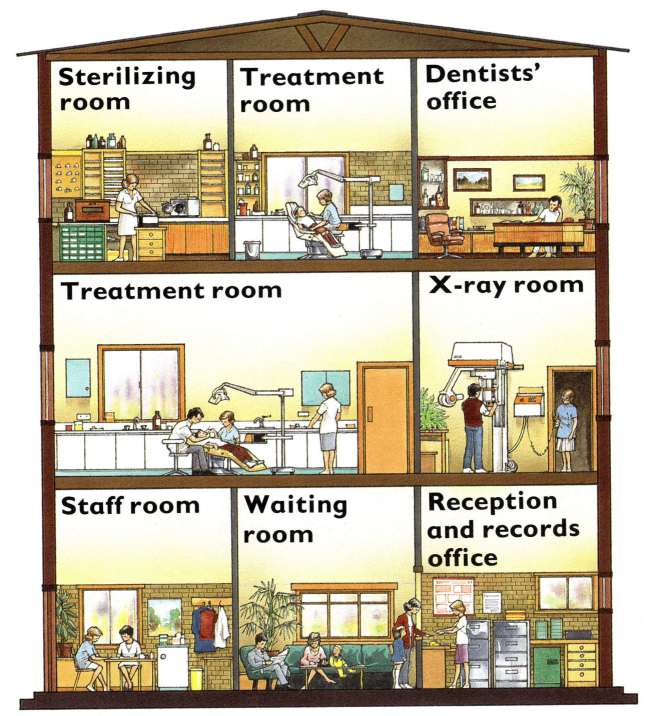

All instruments must be cleaned before use. A machine, called a sterilizer, boils them and kills all the germs.

The nurse lays out the clean instruments for the dentist.

Before she sees a patient, the dentist reads their record card. This reminds her of what treatment the patient has already had.

**This is a new patient.
Her mother must fill in a form for her.**

The dentist comes into the waiting room to meet her new patient.

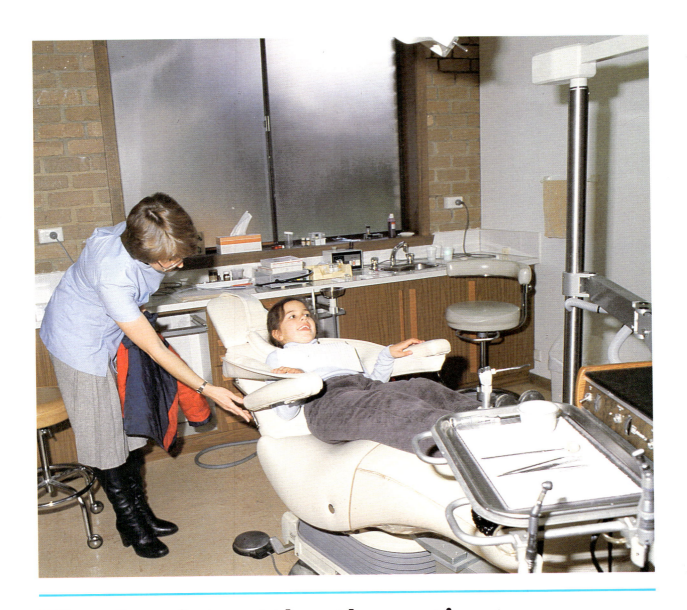

The dentist settles the patient in the chair. The chair can move up and down.

The dentist uses several instruments to examine the patient's teeth.

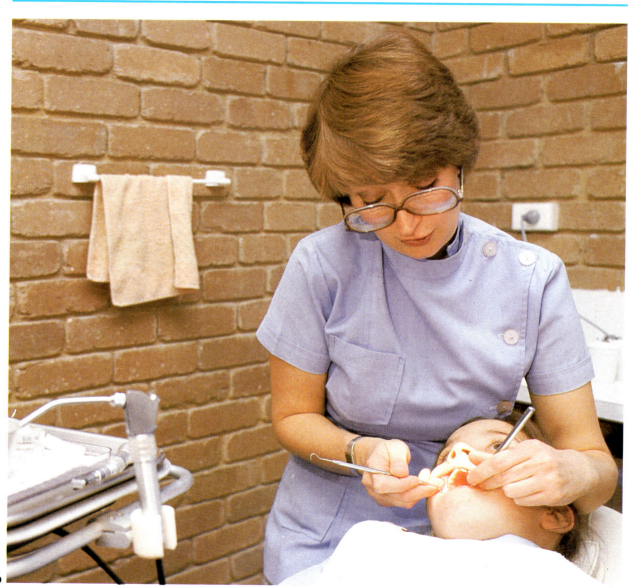

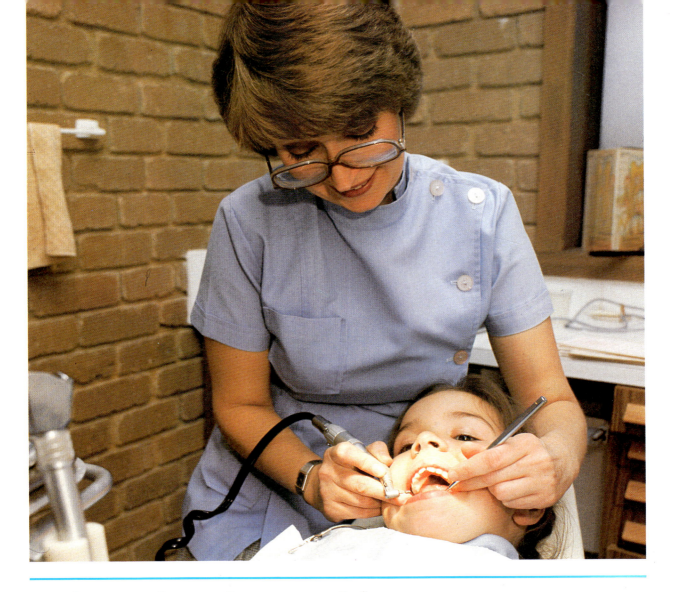

This patient has nothing wrong with her teeth. The dentist just cleans them, using a brush attached to the end of a drill.

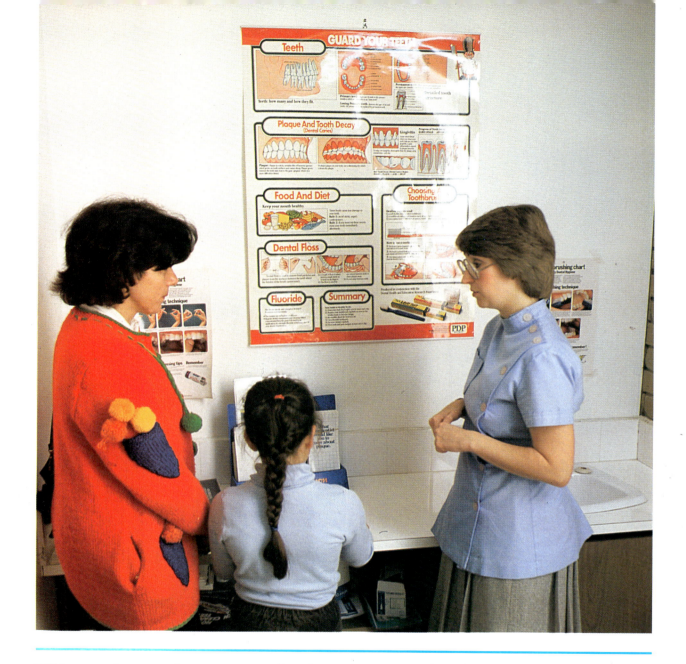

The dentist explains why it is so important to look after teeth.

The nurse shows the patient the correct way to brush teeth. This keeps the gums healthy and helps prevent holes in the teeth.

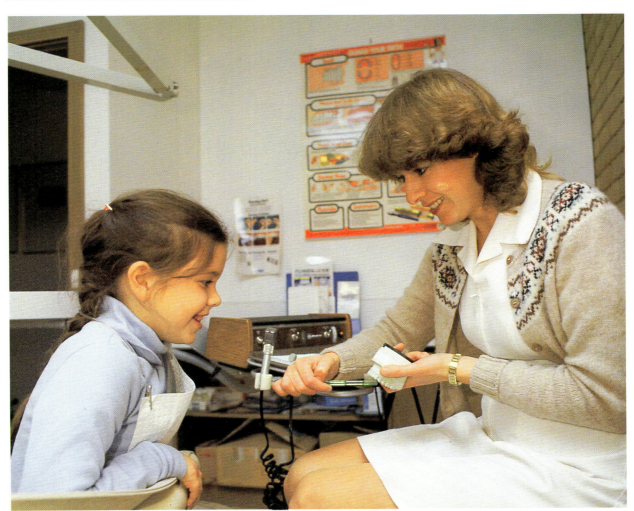

This patient has a hole in one of her teeth. It must be filled. An injection in the gum makes her mouth go numb.

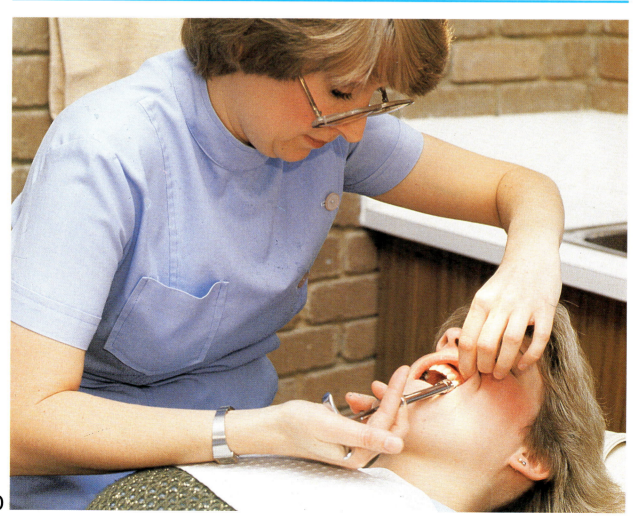

There may be some rotten bits in the hole. This is called decay. The dentist drills it out and makes the hole clean.

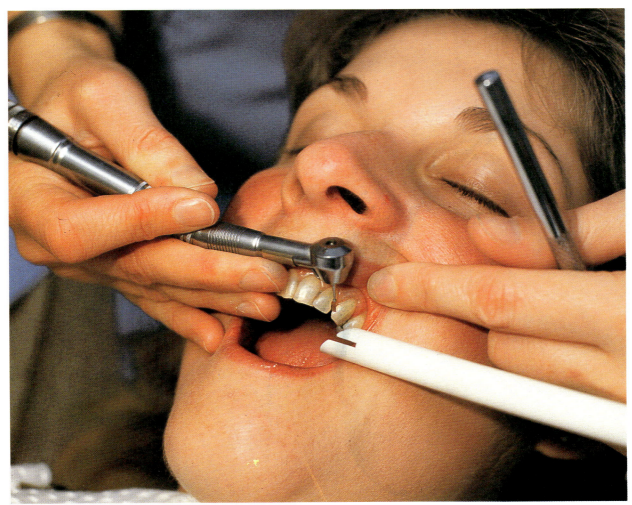

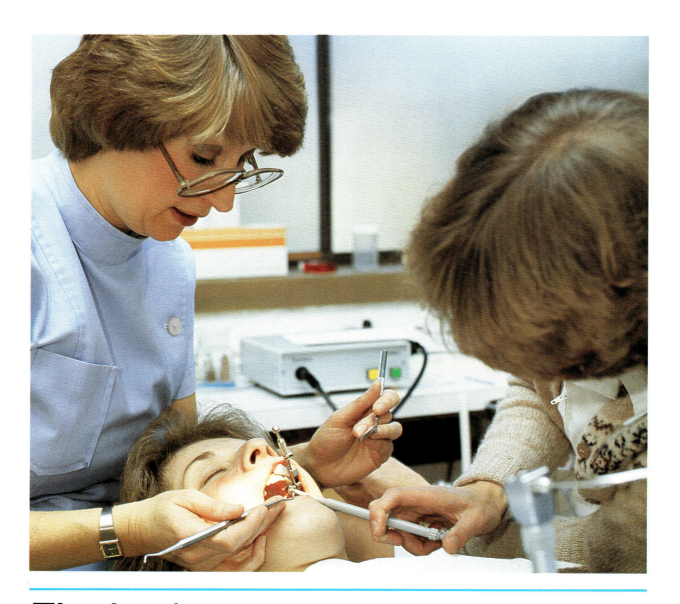

The dentist packs the filling into the hole she has drilled. The filling goes hard very quickly.

This patient has crooked teeth.
The dentist has made a brace.
The strong wires will make
the patient's teeth grow correctly.

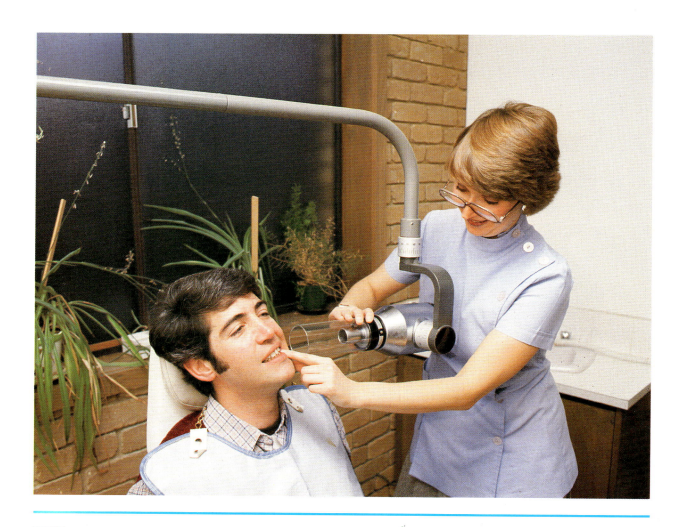

The dentist uses an X-ray machine to take a picture of the inside of this patient's mouth. The picture will show any hidden holes or infection.

**One tooth must be taken out.
An injection is given first.
The dentist pulls the tooth out
without any pain or problems.**

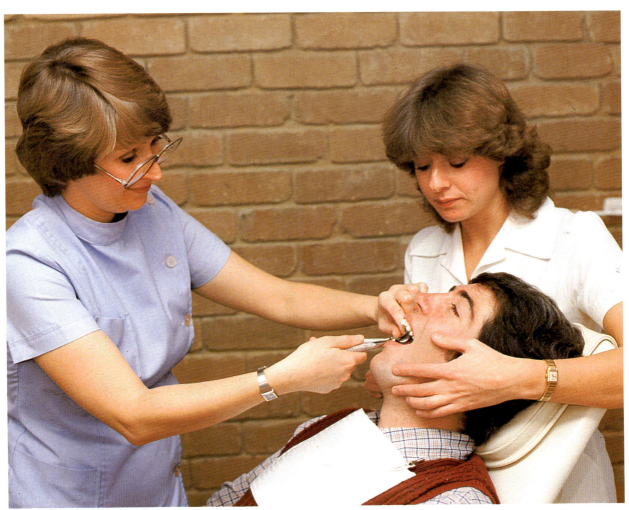

The last patient has gone.
The dentist has time to read
her dental magazines.
She has had a busy day.

FACTS ABOUT TEETH

A human has two sets of teeth. A young child will have about 20 baby teeth. These fall out and the 32 adult teeth grow in their place.

A tooth has two parts — a crown, which is the part you can see, and the roots, which hold the tooth in the mouth.

A chemical called fluoride greatly reduces dental decay. Many brands of toothpaste now contain fluoride. It may also be added to the water supply.

One dentist, who lived a hundred years ago, kept all the teeth he pulled out. At the end of his life he had over 2 million teeth!

Modern dentists try to repair teeth whenever possible, rather than pull them out.

It takes five minutes to clean teeth thoroughly.

Dentists now recommend the use of dental floss, a thin string, to clean between the teeth.

GLOSSARY

Brace
A shape made from wire which is worn in the mouth. It is used to straighten crooked teeth.

Decay
The rotting away of a tooth or part of a tooth.

Drill
The instrument used by the dentist to remove decay from a tooth.

Filling
This is put into a hole in a tooth after the decay has been cleaned out.

Germs
Tiny living things which cause disease.

Gums
The flesh in which the teeth stand.

Sterilizer
A machine which makes instruments free of germs by heating to a very high temperature.

X-ray machine
A machine that takes a picture of the inside of your mouth (or body).

INDEX

Baby teeth 27
Brace 23, 28

Crown 27

Decay 21, 27, 28
Dental floss 27
Dentist's chair 15
Dentists' office 9
Drill 17, 21, 22, 28

Filling 22, 28
Fluoride 27

Germs 10, 28
Gums 19, 20, 28

Infection 24
Injection 20, 25
Instruments 10, 11, 28

Nurse 8, 11, 19

Patient 8, 12, 13, 14, 15, 16, 17, 19, 20, 23, 24, 26

Reception 9
Record cards 8, 12
Records office 9
Roots 27

Staff room 9
Sterilizer 10, 28

Teeth 7, 16, 17, 18, 19, 20, 23, 25, 27, 28
Toothpaste 27

X-ray machine 24, 28

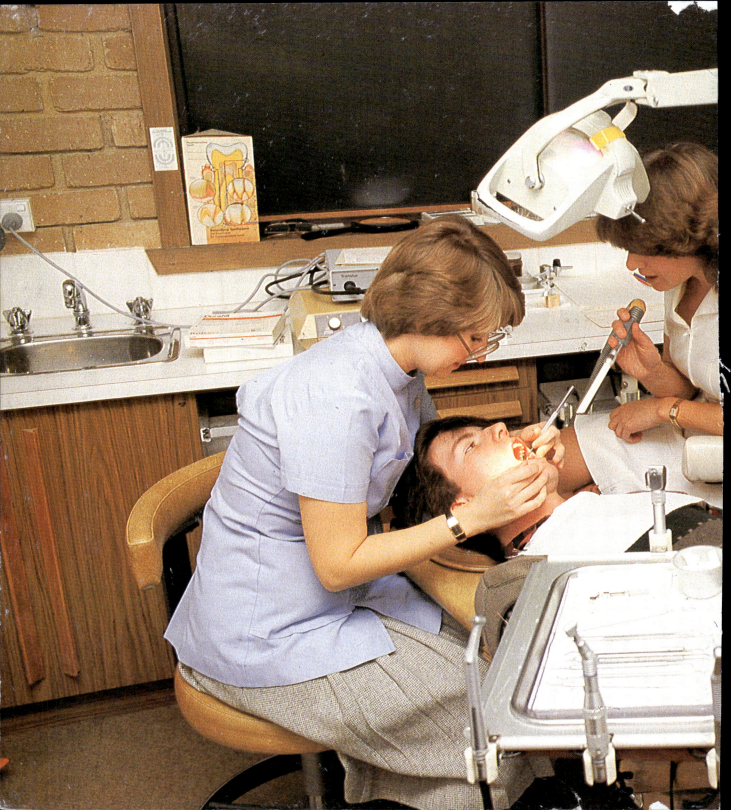